THE FIRST CHRISTMAS

Retold by Anne de Graaf   Illustrated by José Pérez Montero

BROADMAN
&HOLMAN
PUBLISHERS

THE FIRST CHRISTMAS

Published in 1998 by Broadman & Holman Publishers,
Nashville, Tennessee

Text copyright © 1998 Anne de Graaf
Illustration copyright © 1998 José Pérez Montero
Design by Ben Alex
Conceived, designed and produced by Scandinavia Publishing House

Printed in Singapore
ISBN 0-8054-1784-2

The Christmas story begins with a girl named Mary who woke up to a bright light one night. An angel told her, "Mary, you are very special. God has chosen you to become the mother of Jesus, God's Son."

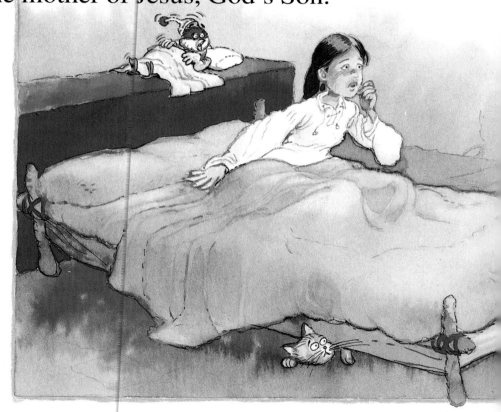

Mary was going to marry
Joseph. When she told
him about her baby,
he shook his head.
"I don't
understand."

God sent an angel to Joseph in a dream. The angel said, "Don't be afraid to make Mary your wife. She is telling the truth about the baby. You will call Him Jesus."

THAT'S who Christmas is about. Baby Jesus.

12

When it was almost time for Jesus to be born, Mary and Joseph had to make a long trip. Mary rode a donkey all the way from Nazareth to Bethlehem.

Jesus was growing in Mary's tummy. Do you know anyone who is going to have a baby? You can pray for that baby now.

When Mary and Joseph arrived in Bethlehem, there was no place for them to stay! The city was full of people. Everywhere they tried, they heard the same thing: "No room!"

What does the donkey say? What does the cow say?

Poor Mary and Joseph! They had to spend the night somewhere. Baby Jesus was going to be born soon! Then they heard about a cave on the edge of town, a stable of sorts. But it was warm and dry.

On the night Jesus was born, shepherds in the nearby hills saw angels singing in the sky, "Glory to God! A Savior was born

tonight!" The shepherds said, "Look at the angels!

found a stable, two people and a tiny,
newborn baby.

Look out your window. How big is the biggest star?

That night the shepherds ran to a
cave in the hillside. Inside, they

Mary and Joseph took Baby Jesus to the temple. An old man named Simeon blessed Jesus. He said, "Now I have seen the Light who will save all people." An old woman named Anna said, "Yes, He is the Savior."

What is Jesus called here?

Three wise men who lived far away from Bethlehem saw the giant star. They rode their camels a long way to find out what the bright star meant. They called Baby Jesus the King of the Jews.

Lie down under a Christmas tree and squint your eyes. Do the lights look like stars?

Were the presents more important than the baby?

These three wise men brought
Jesus fantastic gifts fit for a king.
They gave Jesus gold, and a rich

perfume called myrrh, and
incense, which smells sweet
when burned.

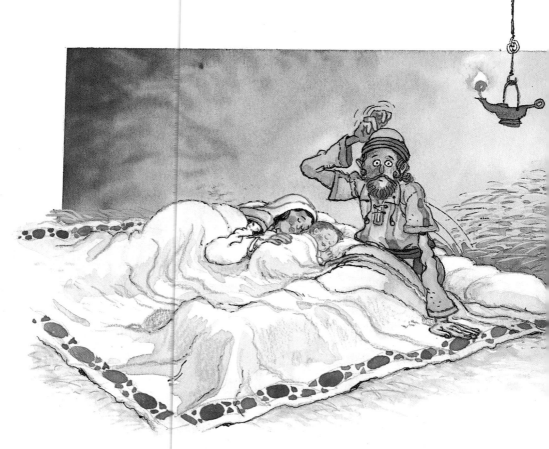

Soon after this, Joseph had a
strange dream. He heard God
say, "King Herod wants to kill
the baby. Run away to Egypt."

When you are scared, where do you run? Give the person reading this book a big hug. Now you're safe.

It was a dark night when Herod wanted to kill Baby Jesus. Where does hope come from?

That very night Joseph did as God asked. He woke up Mary and told her about his dream. "We must listen to God and leave right away." They left that same night for Egypt and kept Jesus safe.

Jesus is the Light who helps us see, the Light who shows us the Way. THAT's who Christmas is about. Baby Jesus.

Jesus is called the Light of the World. On this first Christmas, He was God's Christmas present to us.

37

A NOTE TO THE Big PEOPLE:

The *Little Children's Bible Books* may be your child's first introduction to the Bible, God's Word. In *The First Christmas*, detailed illustrations make the first two chapters of the Gospels of Luke and Matthew spring to life. This is a DO book. Point things out and ask your child to find, seek, say, and discover.

Before you read these stories, pray that your child's little heart would be touched by the love of God. These stories are about planting seeds, having vision, learning right from wrong, and choosing to believe.

A little something fun is said in italics by the narrating animal, to make the story come alive. In this DO book, wave, wink, hop, moo, or do any of the other things the stories suggest so this can become a fun time of growing closer. Pray together after you read this. There's no better way for big people to learn from little people.